THE NORTH
NORFOLK RAILWAY

MARTIN W. BOWMAN

HALSGROVE

First published in Great Britain in 2008

British Library Cataloguing-in-Publication Data
A CIP record for this title is available from the British Library

ISBN 978 1 84114 711 6

HALSGROVE
Halsgrove House,
Ryelands Industrial Estate,
Bagley Road, Wellington, Somerset TA21 9PZ
Tel: 01823 653777 Fax: 01823 216796
email: sales@halsgrove.com
website: www.halsgrove.com

Printed and bound by D'Auria Industrie Grafiche, Italy

INTRODUCTION

Small boys of all ages, it is said, want to be engine drivers. Trains never really made the same lasting impression on me that the 'jet age' did. In the early 1960s I vaguely remember day trips to Wells-next-the Sea and Great Yarmouth and outings further afield. We always went from Thorpe Station. It was never called Norwich station. These were the days before political correctness, when the sounds of the sixties were easy on the airwaves, and the only foreign footballers came from Wales, Ireland and Scotland. A new 1968 Vauxhall Viva 90 (de luxe!) cost just £744 and your Morris Oxford Traveller came in Trafalgar Blue. Car tyres were only £3 17s 6d in real money. In Norwich in 1968 a modern detached bungalow', just three years old, was 'only' £3,350, while a spacious detached house cost just £750 more. All right, so you were on £14 a week and probably you had to work for two or three months to buy a decent camera. However, if, during school holidays, you stood at the yellow crash gate at RAF Coltishall to witness the English Electric Lightning, the last all-British-fighter aircraft, take off with full reheat, then you too would recall these days with affection. No one can ever take away the vivid memories and the cacophony of sound generated by the twin Avons that reverberated around the airfield at take off time like a violent storm.

In literature and on the cinema screen however, steam locos have always been a fascination for me and they conjure up early childhood nostalgia. Enid Blyton's *Famous Five* usually travelled by steam train on their school 'hols' to Kirrin Island. In 1936 W. H. Auden penned *Night Mail* and I remember seeing it on black and white TV when I was a lad in the 1950s. Other perennial favourites include Reverend F. W. Awdry. *The Little Train* was published in 1945 and his more famous *Thomas the Tank Engine* followed a year later. Today *Thomas* and his friends are as popular in books and on the small screen as they ever were. TV regularly shows Alfred Hitchcock's *The 39 Steps*. Its most enduring imagery is of Robert Donat's train steaming across the Forth Rail Bridge where he jumps from the train to escape his pursuers. Hitchcock combined the now-famous sound edit of the landlady's scream as she finds the body in Hannay's flat linked with the shot of the train carrying Hannay towards his adventures in Scotland. The landlady's scream replaced the locomotive whistle and connected the two scenes, adding shock value. Then there's 'Noel Coward's *Brief Encounter* with the unforgettable Celia Johnson and Trevor Howard – which was not so much steamy sex but steam and sex.

It's never been my cup of tea (the film that is) but then nothing will ever compare with *The Dam Busters* at the Noverre or *Zulu* at the Odeon. But I watched avidly from the 'one and nines' *The Train, Northwest Frontier* and that epic of all epics, *Lawrence of Arabia*. Not much in the way of aircraft but a lot of trains bit the dust like those cowboys in the westerns as they were derailed into the nearest ravine or simply blown to smithereens.

Afternoons at the 'pictures' in the so-called 'Swinging Sixties' and balmy days watching the electrifying Lightnings have long gone, but since the dawn of the new century I have rekindled my love affair with all things English Electric. Although who could have foreseen that it would be the English Electric's of the railways and the EE-engined diesels? Once these smelly, faded blue monsters pulled coaches from Norwich Thorpe to Liverpool Street for tedious weekday meetings 'down' in London – otherwise known as 'The Smoke'. The infuriating loco change from diesel to electric at Ipswich was irritatingly time-consuming while for second class travellers like me the British Rail breakfast in the 'First Class' dining car was the only plus.

Bad memories have faded away and the transformation is now complete. Riding shotgun in the cab at the sharp ends (or rather, bull-nosed ends) of the English Electric's is almost as exciting as being a jump-seater on a flight-deck. Imagine my surprise and delight to discover that one innocuous (to me) steam loco is one of the Battle of Britain Class locomotives that salute the memory of the 'Few'. Closer inspection of the malachite green machine revealed its nameplate as *92 Squadron* who in the 1960s flew the English Electric Lightning! But wait, 92 were known then as 'Shiny Blue'!

Most memorable is the steam engine footplate experience. Swaying on unsteady legs, swinging a camera like a nervous hitter at the plate behind perspiring drivers and firemen, inhaling sulphur and steam clouds and sucking in the same beguiling odour of engines, lubricants and the metals and wood that aircraft have, is a vintage cocktail to delight the senses.

Britain, once the workshop of the world, which designed and built innovative 'planes, trains and automobiles' for the Empire, et al, may no longer be the powerhouse it once was but our engineering heritage is second to none. Nostalgia is alive and well and the locomotives are without doubt the best of the 'Best of British'!

Martin W. Bowman
Norwich, 2008

The Muckleburgh Collection

Golf Club

'one' railway Bittern Line Station

Weybourne Mill

Dead Man's Cutting

SHERINGHAM

A149

THE NORTH NORFOLK RAILWAY

Sheringham Park

WEYBOURNE

Kelling Heath Halt

HOLT

ACKNOWLEDGEMENTS

Many unsung heroes and heroines have helped make this book possible, not least the redoubtable drivers and firemen of the engines who always found the room and patience for me. It has been an absolute pleasure and thrill to ride with them on the footplate. In particular I would like to thank Hugh Harkett, Managing Director of the NNR; Tony Lambert, NNR Operating Superintendent; Peter Adds; Alastair Layzell Colonial Pictures Co.; NNR General Manager, Geoff Gowing; fellow aerial photographer Mike Page; Chrissie Rayment, NNR Commercial Manager; Ray Webb and last but not least, Karen Binaccioni for her patience with the page layouts.

THE NORTH NORFOLK RAILWAY

'The public grumble at present-day services and charges, but there is another side to the picture as well... and while we agree that much improvement is needed... the railway has played a big part in the development of Norfolk these past forty years.'

The Norfolk Chronicle, 25 February 1921

In America the iron horse is acknowledged as having opened up the Wild West. In England in the early 1800s steam train companies such as the 'Great Northern' and 'The Midland' were largely coal lines but their omnipotent chairmen were tending towards passenger traffic eastwards. Lord Colville and Sir Henry Oakley wanted to get to the East Coast resorts as an outlet for their teeming millions, so they turned their attentions to parochial Norfolk, which offered great potential and profit for their burgeoning empires. In what were for the majority, very hard times, men of all ages in towns and villages along the routes welcomed this major source of employment. Melton Constable, for instance, would grow up around the M&GN's locomotive and wagon works and come to be known as 'the Crewe of North Norfolk'. William Marriott, Engineer and Traffic Manager, M&GN Joint Railway, called one of the new streets in Melton Constable after Lord Colville. He regarded his lordship 'as such a fine specimen of the English gentleman', that it was often said that 'we should consider it an honour to black his boots'. Such were the days when the *hoi polloi* doffed their caps in the presence of their guv'nors and royal personages. King Edward the Prince of Wales and other titled travellers like the Duke of Clarence and Empress Frederick travelled in the style of the characters in *Murder on the 'Orient Express*, even if it was only by train to South Lynn and Aylsham. Marriott, who worked for the M&GN and its predecessors from 1880 until retirement at the end of 1924 and who held the posts of engineer from 1883 and loco superintendent from 1884, often met the aristocracy, whose entourage included 'Poirot-style' characters like Inspector Conquest of Scotland Yard. In addition to his other responsibilities, Marriott was appointed traffic manager in January 1919. He made No.8 Cromer Road, Sheringham, overlooking the station, his summer residence and he used an old carriage in the garden as a summer house. On 8 August 1973 Sir Robert Marriott unveiled on the wall of the house, a plaque to the memory of his father, in effect the 'architect' of the new line to the North Norfolk coast.

In 1880 the rails reached Holt but the line had not been ballasted, some of the banks were not in order or had not been finished and nothing had been done to the station yard. Marriott obtained a moderate sum of money from the directors and had an old wooden station brought from Yarmouth and built a sleeper platform. Finally, on 1 October 1884 the branch line from Melton Constable opened to Holt. In 1887 the station at Sheringham was built for the opening of the line, which continued to Cromer in June that same year. William Marriott recalled that the line was very interesting to make and observed that 'there were people in Sheringham who had never yet seen a locomotive. Old Granny Craske was got into a bath chair and taken to the level crossing to see her first engine.' The engineer had the 'warmest recollections of the kindness' extended to him by both the Squires of Sheringham and Beeston Regis and added that the fisherman in those days 'were splendid men'.

The M&GN became the largest joint railway in Britain, opening up a vast new area for competition with the established railways such as the London North Eastern Railway and the Great Eastern. While they were universally known by their acronyms as the LNER and GER, some said that M&GN stood for 'Muddle and go nowhere'. This was never more so than in August 1944 when slightly puzzled RAF aircrew waited on a platform at a Norwich railway station. Squadron Leader John Crotch and his crew, who had flown twenty operations on Halifax bombers from Holme-on-Spalding Moor, had had enough of 'life' at the bleak Yorkshire air station. Their skipper, who had been a practising solicitor in the city since 1935, had assured them that a posting to Foulsham 'would be good because it was near Norwich'. Crotch told his crew to stay at the Bell Hotel overnight and meet him at the City station the next morning. They left at 10.00 am but the M&GN route involved so many stops that they did not get to Guestwick station until 3 o'clock in the afternoon! The crew said, "Hey Skip, we thought we were going to a base near Norwich!"

On 21 May 1960 passengers returned briefly to Norwich (City) railway station when the M&GN Joint Railway Preservation Society ran a tour covering Norwich and the remains of the Waveney Valley line. The two engines that were used were 'J15' No.65469, a sister loco to the NNR's J15 65462, and the other was the last 'B12' No.61572, which is now part of the NNR's historic rolling stock. Norwich (City) railway station closed on 3 February 1969.

The M&GN was formed on 1 July 1893 and the two partners had equal representation and agreed spheres of responsibility until from 1 October 1936 operation was permanently undertaken by the LNER. The system, which extended from Peterborough and Little Bytham in the west to Yarmouth (Beach), Norwich (City) and Cromer (Beach) in the east, was more than a second route to Norfolk from London (King's Cross). It also provided a valuable conveyance for Midland holidaymakers and day-trippers wishing to travel to Great Yarmouth and Cromer. 'A Regional History of the Railways of Great Britain' records that.

> 'Goods traffic was once fairly substantial and, in the mid-1930s traffic included fish trains from Yarmouth, cattle workings and the movement of grain, beet, manufactured goods from and coal to Norwich, enormous quantities of fruit and produce from the Fens and much general merchandise.'

When the system largely disappeared on 28 February 1959 many passengers travelled dressed in black, complete with arm bands and top hats. One of the last trains bound for Melton Constable was decorated with a laurel wreath on its smokebox and a slogan read: 'Goodbye all: We may not pass this way again'. Even so, passenger services between Sheringham and Melton Constable survived until 4 April 1964.

In 1965 Central Norfolk Enterprises purchased the Sheringham to Weybourne section for £17,000 and began restoring the line. Weybourne station, which stands on a brief stretch of almost level track between two long gradients of 1 in 80, had opened in 1901 and was provided with a crossing loop to break up 6-mile single line section between Holt and Sheringham. In typical rural railway fashion, Weybourne Station is around a mile from the village it serves. Much bigger than the usual Victorian country station, Weybourne was built in anticipation of the village becoming a popular resort but this never materialised. The Weybourne Springs, a large hotel in turreted style built at the turn of the 20th century, was demolished at the outset of the Second World War, as it was thought that it could be used as a landmark by German bombers coming in over the coast. Some compensation was found, however, in the artillery firing range established at Holt from 1936, which provided reasonably extensive military traffic. During both World Wars, the railway brought troops to Weybourne Camp (now the site of the Muckleburgh Collection military museum). Traffic was such that

LNER N7 0-6-2T 69621 casting shadows in the weak January sun paralleling the A149 near Sheringham Golf Course.

Mike Page

Weybourne had a stationmaster, two signalmen and three porters. The up loop was removed following closure of the signal box on 6 June 1961 and by mid-1965 the remaining track had been lifted through the platforms. British Rail removed the entire track and sidings before the M&GN Preservation Society could raise sufficient capital though eventually it was able to raise enough funds to save the three-mile section from Weybourne to the station boundary at Sheringham. Today Weybourne station is licensed for marriages. Alongside are the recently extended locomotive and Carriage & Wagon workshops, one of the few heavy engineering facilities left in Norfolk and successor to the M&GN workshops at Melton Constable.

By the mid-1960s Sheringham station was far too large for British Rail's needs and on 2 January 1967 a new halt was opened on the east side of the level crossing when BR abandoned the original Station. The M&GN Preservation Society immediately took a lease on the station buildings and Central Norfolk Enterprises Ltd was formed. The track over the crossing in Station Road remained in place and on 4 June 1967 it enabled a train of stock to be delivered directly to the infant preservation society, which in 1969 became the North Norfolk Railway Company (NNR). It then went public, initially raising £14,000. During this time volunteers had been relaying the track and sidings ready for locomotives and rolling stock already purchased. These included two steam locomotives, two Diesel Railbuses and a set of four 1924 ex-King's Cross Suburban Quad-art teak-bodied coaches. These unique articulated carriages were designed by Sir Nigel Gresley, the famous railway engine designer who also created the record-breaking Mallard loco, which was years ahead of its time. The Quad-art set, which is the forerunner of the articulated principle used on Eurostar high speed trains, have now been fully restored with the help of a £500,000 rebuild, mainly funded by the Heritage Lottery Fund. On 13 July 1975 the line from Sheringham to Weybourne was finally opened. Sheringham station now looks the way it would have appeared during British Railways days in the 1950s and its restoration has won a Heritage Railways Association award. Since 1976 the NNR has been wholly responsible for the operation of the railway. Single track was laid southwest from Weybourne to Kelling Camp Halt (reached in August 1983) and Holt. The original 1887 Holt station disappeared with the building of a town bypass so in 1988 the NNR built its own station about one mile short of the original, just off the A148 Cromer-Fakenham road. The station at Holt (High Kelling) is the former M&GN Stalham station, built in 1878 and re-erected and reopened a century and a quarter later.

The Society owns four historic steam locomotives, a Class 31 diesel and a number of important heritage carriages and wagons. In 2006 the Society opened the William Marriott Museum at Holt Station. The NNR has around 30 paid staff while the Society's 2,000 members come from all walks of life, from all over the country and some even from abroad. They all enjoy sharing in a very special heritage. Clement Scott, a journalist and poet who visited the area in Victorian times and christened it 'Poppyland' popularised the area through his column in the *Daily Telegraph* and the railway was its lifeline, bringing thousands of visitors each year to its unspoiled countryside and magnificent beaches. Views of the coast and countryside along the 5½-mile line from Sheringham to Weybourne and through the heathland to Holt are as breathtaking as ever. The NNR is one of Britain's top five heritage railways, carrying over 125,000 passengers a year on one of the most scenic steam heritage railways in Britain.

The prestigious B12/3 4-6-0 locomotive in its LNER Apple Green livery in April 1995. This Holden-designed Class B.12/3 was built in 1928 for express work and it is now the only working inside-cylinder 4-6-0 in Europe. 8572 was the running number for the M&GN Joint Railway Society owned locomotive when it was running in LNER. It was repainted in its more usual BR livery and its running number reverted to 61572.

B.12/3 No.61572 4-6-0 climbing the 1 in 80 gradient near High Kelling. After more than 30 years in retirement this engine was returned to steam in 1995 following a protracted restoration project and rebuilding at a steam loco works in former East Germany.

B.12/3 No.61572 4-6-0 steaming out from under bridge 302 at Weybourne station. 4-6-0 refers to the arrangement of the driving wheels on locomotives, ie four at the front, six main and none at the rear before the tender.

B.12/3 No.61572 4-6-0 running majestically along the line near High Kelling approaching the ex-M&GN somersault distant signal at Weybourne. Some signals in the 1870s were operated with a signal arm fixed inside a slotted post. One such became frozen into its slot and the false indication caused a serious accident in 1876. Edward French of the GNR was motivated by this event to solve the problem with a centre balanced, or somersault, arm.

B.12/3 No.61572 4-6-0 passing the somersault signal near High Kelling.

The cab

92 Squadron on the line near Upper Sheringham in September 2004

Under the canopy at Sheringham station the original stanchions, and the spandrels cast into them, contrast with modern electric lightning.

British Type 2 31 207, which is like the pushmepullyou in *Doctor Dolittle*, in that all diesel locomotives have a No.1 and a No.2 end. The No.1 end on British Railways diesel locomotives is always the radiator end, which is denoted by the large grills on each side of the body.

Pulling into Weybourne Station in the Class 31 207 diesel loco.

DMU waiting patiently at Weybourne.

Opposite: The main coast road runs alongside the railway for a while after leaving Upper Sheringham. Over the golf course, extensive views of the North Sea appear once the train has passed Skelding Hill with its small white (formerly Coastguard) hut on the top. Mike Page

DMU (Diesel multiple unit) en route to Holt viewed from Kelling Heath. The railway climbs sharply at 1 in 80 from Weybourne up to Holt (who said Norfolk was flat?) passing Kelling Halt where steam trains stop by request, but only on the downhill journey towards Sheringham. So steep is the gradient, only diesel railcars are permitted to call at this request stop in the westbound direction as heavier, locomotive-hauled trains might experience difficulties re-starting.

After operating between Sheringham and Weybourne for several years, the North Norfolk Railway extended their diesel railbus service to Kelling Camp Halt in late August 1983. The original rudimentary boarding place was improved and renamed Kelling Heath Park by the time services to Holt were restored. The steam or diesel hauled trains are only able to stop in the Weybourne direction due to the gradient.

After the Golf Course the line from Sheringham enters a natural cleft in the fields of barley carrots and sugar beet. The track levels out for a short before passing under bridge 304 before descending at 1–in–100 in a cutting through Dead Man's Hill where local legend has is that the victims of the Great Plague from Weybourne were buried remote from their homes. Mike Page

Biggin on the Bump. No.34081 'Battle of Britain Class' with the *Biggin Hill* numberplate replacing that of *92 Squadron* steaming up Kelling Bank.

No.90775 on the line below Kelling Heath.

NNR's steam locos use over 2,000 litres of water during the round trip from Sheringham to Holt and back – equivalent to 30 bathsfull of water. Steam engines take water from the water column on platform 2, built to an E&MR design dating back to the 1880s and crafted in the railway's own workshops. No plans could be found so the NNR looked to old pictures and started from there. The leather delivery bag is 6m long and held together by dozens of copper rivets. Three other columns have been built along the railway.

TV personality Annabel Croft visited the North Norfolk Railway during the making of the TV series *The Flying Picnic*, which was based on an Edwardian picnic by Mrs Beeton except that Annabel flew around the county of Norfolk in a Tiger Moth, stopping off at places along the way. At Sheringham she boiled a kettle on the footplate (or should it be hotplate?) and was served tea and scones in the First Class carriage. (Colonial Pictures Co)

Sheringham bracing itself against the onslaught of fierce November winds, waves and white horses pounding the shoreline. The railway line heads (left) towards the Golf Course under 305, which carries Church Street into the town. Immediately after bridge 305 on the south side of the line is a replica M&GN style water tower built in 2003. On the seaward side is the Sheringham West signal box. Opposite are the original carriage sidings from BR and M&GN days where stock not in use is stored. On 8 August 1973 Sir Robert Marriott unveiled a plaque on the wall of No.8 Cromer Road to the memory of his father William, Engineer and Traffic Manager, M&GN Joint Railway, whose summer house faced the station across what is now the car park.

Sheringham station was built for the opening of the line in 1887 and British Rail continued to use the station until the spring of 1967 when they built a wooden halt on the Cromer side of the level crossing on Station Road. The station is now restored to the way it would have looked during the 1950s. It is hoped to re-erect the missing buildings and canopies at Sheringham that BR demolished in the 1960s. And as the locos run round their trains at the station, they come almost face to face with their modern counterparts at the Sheringham terminus of the Bittern line to Norwich. Sheringham (originally spelt with the double rr) is a charmingly typical English seaside resort, busy and bustling throughout the season.

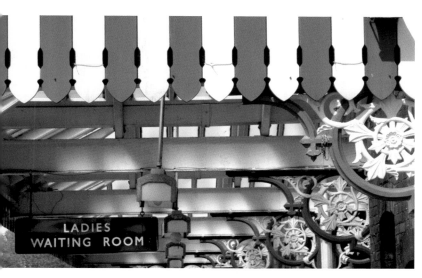

Canopy over Platform 1 at Sheringham.

M&GN JR fire buckets at Sheringham.

Sheringham station from Bridge 305, which carries Church Street into the town centre. When the station was built in 1887 it stood in open countryside and Sheringham was a small fishing village. With the arrival of the railway, tourism flourished and many houses were built around the station although original flint cottages are still to be seen at the seaward end of the town. Fishermen still go to sea for lobsters and crabs in a small fleet of boats, which can be seen drawn up the gently sloping beach when not in use. The station began as a typical M&GN 'hall and cross wings' building and grew with the town that it served until it became what it is today.

Opposite: Leaving Sheringham the train crosses Sweetbriar Lane automatic level crossing, a private road that leads to Sheringham Golf Club. Landward, in the distance, is the attractive flint-walled village and church of Upper Sheringham, nestling in the wooded hills. Deposits of morainic materials (sands, gravels, clays, and flints) left behind when the ice sheets of the Ice Age melted formed the hills of this area of Norfolk. Mike Page

Leaving Sheringham and after passing under bridge 304 an embankment carries the track to bridge 303 over the A149. Mike Page

Bridge 303 carrying the line over the A149 coast road was strengthened in 1984 and a 5mph speed restriction resulting from the poor condition of the bridge was finally lifted. David James Pinkerton, a professional railwayman working as a volunteer, died in an accidental fall on 30 October 1984 when the bridge was almost completed. A plaque built into its abutment is a lasting monument to his dedication.

Alongside Weybourne station are the locomotive and Carriage & Wagon workshops. In the late 1970s the NNR re-erected the engine shed from Norwich City station and it has been considerably extended by the addition of a machine shop and part of the former March Diesel Depot as a dedicated carriage and wagon workshop.

D6732, an English Electric Class 37 Type 3 diesel locomotive under restoration at Weybourne. When completed its coat of Brunswick Green and inner workings will be as good as the day it was built in 1960 at the Vulcan Foundry in Newton-le-Willows.

But is it art? One of the rolling stock items is a former Wisbech & Upwell tramway coach whose sister carriage starred in the famous Ealing comedy *The Titfield Thunderbolt*, the first Ealing Studios comedy in Technicolor when it appeared in March 1953. The antique 'Thunderbolt' is raided from the local museum when the coach company proprietors wreck the original train. The tramway coach was complete with a saloon bar for an alcoholic named Valentine, a well to do philanthropist played by Stanley Holloway. Valentine is a local eccentric and a man of leisure who spends all his time in the pub. As the bar on a train does not have to observe pub closing times, he helps save the line from extinction. The same could not be said of the coach, which after filming was broken up. The surviving carriage had been faithfully restored by NNR, who not to be outdone, installed a replica bar! The Gresley buffet car No.51769 originally built by the LNER at York is also in 1st class condition after restoration.

B12/3 4-6-0 No.61572 at Sheringham.

The WD at Holt in spring snow. The WD, which spent 40 years abroad working in Egypt and Greece, was the M&GN Society's fourth steam engine, which was purchased in 2006 and had been on hire to the NNR for the previous three years.

The railway line between Sheringham and Holt is single-track with a passing loop at Weybourne and is controlled by signal boxes. There are no turntables at either end of the line. If more than one train were to use a single line section of track at the same time, it could prove disastrous. On the night of 10 September 1874 during a very heavy rainstorm a mail train and an express were involved in a head-on crash at Thorpe on the single line between Norwich and Brundall. Both drivers and the two firemen and 15 passengers died and more than 30 people were injured. In 1878 methods were introduced to ensure that at any given time one train only could enter onto a single line section of railway and the 'tablet' and 'train staff'' are the safety devices used by the NNR. The tablet is a metal disc, which must be used when the locomotive is travelling between two signal boxes. The driver surrenders the tablet to the signalman who inserts it into the 'Tyers No.6' instrument, which provides a mechanical communication for the signalmen who control that section. The instrument allows the signalman to unlock the levers, so that he can 'clear' the signal (from 'stop' to 'go') to allow the locomotive driver to proceed safely. Before the signal box was opened at Holt, a 'train staff''(a small slab of aluminium with a brass 'key' at each end), was carried by the footplate crew to unlock the 'ground frame'. This is a set of points used by driver to run his locomotive around to the opposite end of the train. Thus the steam locomotives 'pull' their trains 'chimney first' to Holt and having run round then 'tow' them back to Weybourne and Sheringham. While it is no longer needed to unlock the ground frame, the 'staff''(and the 'tablet') have the name of the section engraved on them and the driver must have in his possession the correct one for that particular section. Other trains wishing to use that same section of single line track have to wait until the 'down' train returns and the 'staff' or the tablet is exchanged.

Nearing Sheringham Ray Webb gets ready to hand over the 'staff' to the signalman at the West box.

The signalman takes the staff.

Journey's end and the engine driver surrenders the pouch to the signalman at Sheringham West box. It is here that the signalman hands to the driver the tablet to enable him to enter the single line section ahead.

The Tyers No.6 apparatus (right) at Sheringham West box where the tablet goes in the pull out tray like a CD player. The staff has been inserted in its instrument (left).

Approaching Weybourne the fireman prepares to take the tablet from the signalman. The tablet is carried in a hooped pouch to facilitate exchanges between driver and signalman when the train is in motion.

The 'tablet' for the single line section between Weybourne and Holt.

Signalman Peter Adds hands the driver of the diesel the 'tablet' as he leaves Sheringham.

Hugh Harkett hands over the 'train staff' for the Weybourne to Holt section to the fireman of 90775 who in turn surrenders the tablet for the Sheringham to Weybourne section.

LNER built Class V2 2-6-2 locomotive 60800 *'Green Arrow'* bound for Weybourne approaching bridge 304 over the A149 on Boxing Day 2004. Built in May 1936 *'Green Arrow'* is owned by the National Railway Museum at York and was on loan to the NNR (and other heritage railways) when its main line 'ticket' had expired. It could continue work on heritage railways until its boiler life dictates that it needs to be withdrawn for overhaul. Mike Page

In 2007 the NNR was privileged to have the most powerful engine ever to be run on the line with the arrival of British Rail Class 9F 2-10-0 No.92203 *Black Prince* which is owned by David Shepherd. The world-renowned wildlife artist and conservationist made his 120-ton heavy freight locomotive available as part of a round-Britain tour of preserved railway lines during which he sought to raise money for his wildlife foundation. The huge loco, which was built at the Swindon Locomotive Works in 1959, was brought from the Gloucestershire and Warwickshire Railway where it usually runs on the back of a low load trailer. David Shepherd saved the historic locomotive from being scrapped in 1967 after he had a successful one-man show in New York. He sold all his pictures in the same day and being impulsive, rang British Rail and bought the engine for the princely sum of £3,000.

Since then he estimates that it has cost him more than £500,000 to maintain. The 9F was the most successful of the BR standard classes and was designed by Robert Riddles. The first 9Fs to emerge from Crewe were allocated to the heavy iron ore workings in South Wales and County Durham. When tried on passenger trains they were capable of running at speeds of up to 90 mph. When construction ended in March 1960, a total of 251 9F locomotives had been built but now there are only five left, only two of which are currently running.

No.60800 The Green Arrow in full flight along the 3-mile section between Sheringham and Weybourne. Mike Page

Thomas the tank engine is always a favourite with the children.

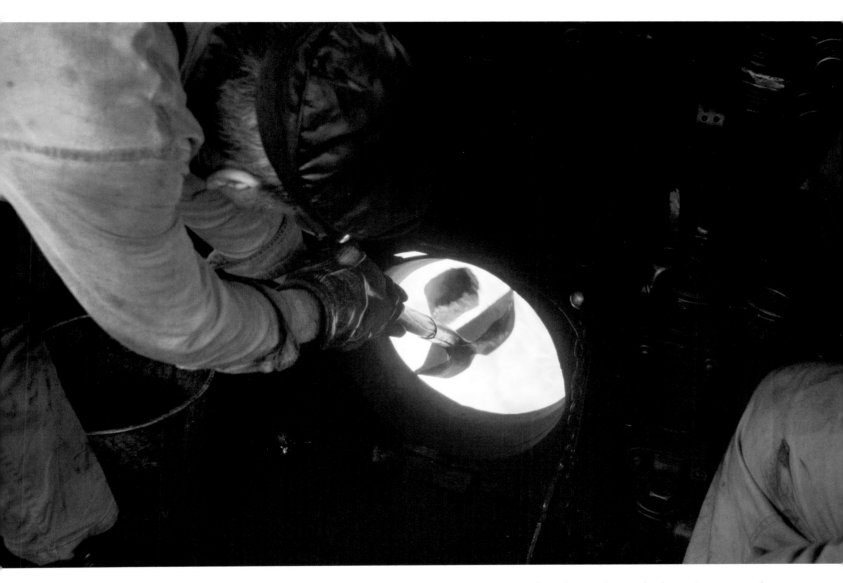

Ray Webb, fireman and a horologist from Suffolk, has been up since 5.30am getting the engine stoked up. A steam train will use between two to three tons of coal per day, depending on the skill of the driver. The uphill part of the line keeps the firemen busy and they have to top up the loco with water at Weybourne.

The B12 has been called the NNR's 'flagship locomotive', built to a Great Eastern Railway design by Beyer Peacock in Manchester in 1928 for express work.

Opposite: Give a little whistle!

R. A. Riddles-designed ex-WD 2-10-0 No.90775 pulling a train near Upper Sheringham. Built in 1943 this engine was acquired in 1945 by Hellenic State Railways and used to haul the Athens-Istanbul Express.

'Johnny'.

Running on time.

61572 approaching Holt.

Levelling off the coal.

92 Squadron 'flying' out of Sheringham station.

A double headed train comprising Class J15 No.65462 0-6-0 tender engine and LBSC 662 approaching Weybourne Station. The line from Sheringham runs through a short cutting before Weybourne Station is reached. On the landward side, the wooded hills continue with showy rhododendrons in late spring and the golden brown of bracken in autumn.

Mike Page

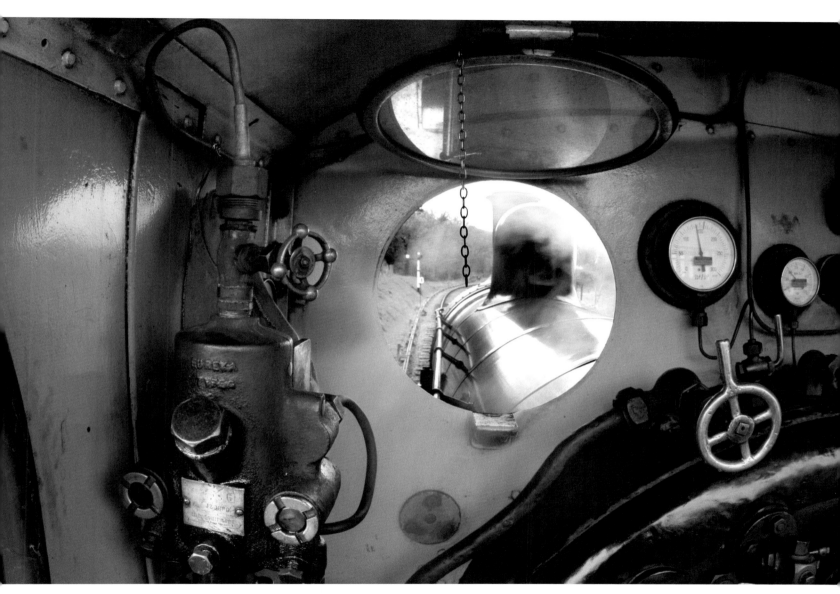

65462 prepares to set off from Weybourne for Holt.

In the workshops at Weybourne.

92 Squadron looking splendid in the late evening June sun.

Didleedum, Didleedum, Didleedum
by MWB (inspired by W.H. Auden)

Didleedum, Didleedum, Didleedum.
Sherrin'hum.
'Holt, here we come'.
Three-forty-one.
Platform 1.
Diddledum, Diddledum
How about that Mum?
Henrietta?
Get her.
All aboard!
Nothing untoward?
Wait.
Brake?
3.43.
Fiddily-dee, Fiddily-dee.
WD? Type 23?
Didleedee, didleedee, didleedee.

Now standing at two.
Crewe?
4-6-2?
2-ten-zero?
Hellenic Hero!
Going loco,
Down in Alcapulco.
0-6-0?
Hornby Double O.
Runs like clockwork, turn the key.
Narrow gauge.
All the rage.
Bogies flexing.
Vicars Vexing.
Class 37.
Western?
English Electric.
How eclectic.
Chattanooga Choo Choo, Hunslet, Riddles and spike
Malachite?
Right!
Be specific. Could be a *Pacific*.
Brunswick Green.
Tan and cream.
Get up steam!
Live that dream.
Holden
Beholdin'

5197 built by the Lima Locomotive Works.

In the early 1900s most US companies bought their new locomotives from Alco, Baldwin or Lima. In 1921 orders for Lima built locos had dried up and the works virtually shut down. It had grown on the building of the specialised patent 'Shay' geared locomotives, for logging lines but in 1916 had hired a new design chief, William E. Woodard, from Alco and went for a share of the 'Class One' market – the big main-line railroads. Lima ceased building steam locos in 1949.

Awdry, Auden, Gordon,
Thomas the tank-Toby the Tram-Bertie the bus -
   huffers and puffers.
Mind the buffers.
Doggies.
Moggies.
Station bat.
Bowler hat.
Fat
controller,
Got a Roller?
'Duck' and the diesel engine.
Worth a mention.
'Edward's' blue.
'Annie &'Clarabel' too.
Ticketyboo.
'Jimmy's' red.
'Ollie's in the shed.
Percy's small.
High Speed haul.
'Henry's' Green.
Always serene.
'Emily's' available.
'Stepney's' a 'Bluebell'.
Dingley-Dell, Dingley-Dell.
Trainee?
Didleedee, didleedee, didleedee

Ready?
Steady.
Sir Nigel Gresley.
Casey
Jones the driver,
For Welsh Ivor,
Harriet
Marriott,
Stephenson's Rocket.
Fix that sprocket.
Great Eastern, Western too.
Pushmepullyou.
That'll never do.
Beeching, Far reaching.
Bit off more than he could choo.
Bittern, Britten,
Bulleid's plight,
Trainspotters' delight.
Men of Kent's 92.
'Shiny Blue'.
Classy act -
fact.

Peter the fireman

92 Squadron showing its class.

The Green Arrow caught in a colourful time warp two days after Christmas 2004. Mike Page

Opposite: LNER N7 0-6-2T 69621 leaving Weybourne from under bridge 302.

Battle of Britain class -
Fast!
Never doubt her.
Brief Encounter.
Sex and steaming.
Howard, and Celia leaving.
On the 5.43.
Tweedledee,
Tweedledum.
Didleedee, didleedum.

Wheeltappers, flappers & snappers,
Goin' like the clappers.
Firemen's footplate -
Grate!
Smokebox.
Pull up your socks.
Lots to do.
Who met his Waterloo?
Napoleon.
Linoleum.
Booking Hall floor,
To the door.
Guards in the van.
Signalman.
Flying Scot
Running hot.
Golden Arrow,
Straight and narrow
Shunters and shakers,
Movers and makers,
Holidaytakers.
Day trippers,
City slickers.
Inspector, director.
Don't forget her.
Just the ticket at the wicket.
Booking clerks.
Watch for sparks.
Under the clock.
Look for the frock.
Your goal?
That buttonhole,
Carnation?
Assignation-Perspiration-Consternation!
She's out of town, I'll be bound.
Doom and gloom.
Waiting room.
Sweeper's broom.
Sooty and sweep.

The initials of the Eastern and Midlands Railway are seen intertwined in the ornamental ironwork supporting the platform seat at Sheringham station. The E&MR was an amalgamation of the Lynn and Fakenham Railway with the Great Yarmouth and Stalham Light. The GN and MR jointly took over the E&MR from 1 July 1893.

Watch your feet.
Fenchurch Street.
That's the beat.
Let us meet.
Stand and greet.
London Liverpool Street.
Haven't you heard?
Got the bird?
First, Second and Third.
Just a single.
What a mingle.
Platform Nine.
Just in time.
There's the train.
Off again.
Night Mail.
Blowing a gale.
Wind and rain
What a pain.
Doing the rounds.
Essex towns.
Manningtree.
Didleedee, didleedee, didleedee.
Boat train for the Hook.
Look.
Change for Harwich.
Take your carriage.
Too much baggage.
Milk train.
Mind that urn.
No return.

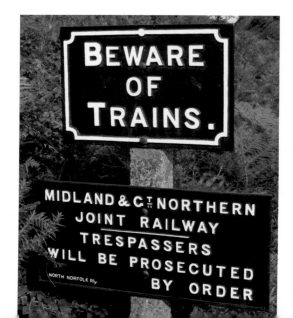

Ipswich and Diss.
Hiss.
Well trained.
Home again.
Norwich Thorpe.
Time warp.
Coast Express.
No distress.
Yarmouth (Beach),
Out of reach.
Norfolk coast,
That's the toast.
Poppyland,
And?
Doing fine.
Didleedine, didleedine, didleedine.

Poppy Line.
On time.
Bridge 299.
Nein!
Past the 149.
Track 29?
Whistle, Water, Wave the flag,
Put out that fag.
Water tower, Windmill Crossing,
Keep you a troshin'
Single track, nutty slack, back to back.
...Leaving... steam–ing ...believing...
...Shunt-ing... chugg–ing... lugging...
hugg–ing,
Sleeping-dreaming-gleaming-revealing.
Runs on wheels.
Quick on its heels.
Chasing, chasing,
Times a wastin'
Going far?
Take the Dining car.
M&GN,
When?
LMS – best?
British Rail?
On the nail!
EMR
LNER,
NNR –
Better by far!
Eastern Region;
They were legion.
Never humdrum.
Didleedum, didleedum, didleedum.

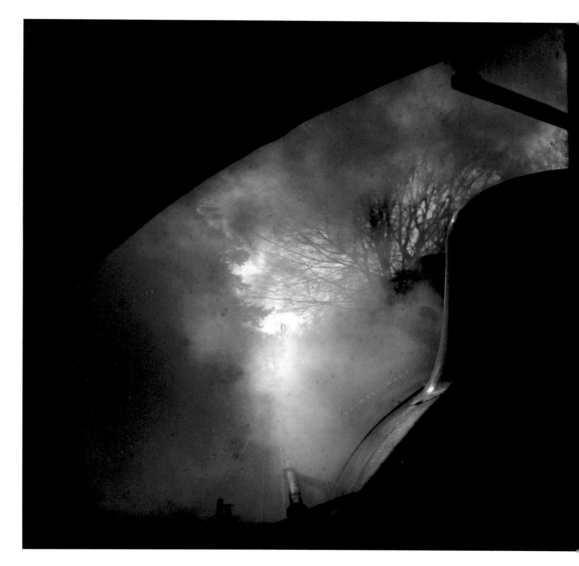

The original signal box at Sheringham station, a lofty structure providing an unobstructed view over the station buildings, was replaced in 1906 by two new boxes, 'East' and 'West' to cope with additional traffic. BR demolished the sheringham West box in 1965 to prevent vandalism and in 1980 the former wens um Junction Box at Norwich Thorpe was acquired to replace it. The lever frame came from Loughlin on the Central Line (previously the GER) and was the last mechanical signal box on the London Underground. The colours of the levers are as follows: Red, signals; Black, points; Blue, facing point locks; White, spare; Brown/blue, locking level control ground frame.

Weybourne station signal box and the arrival of 61572 whose driver has his tablet ready for the Tyers No.6 apparatus by the window.

Array of levers in the Weybourne Signal Box.

The signal box at Weybourne was relocated from Holt in 1967 to replace the original box, which was demolished by BR in 1964 along with the waiting room on this platform. It was recommissioned in 1989 following a lengthy overhaul and it allows the NNR to run a more intensive service for passengers.

Opposite: At Sheringham station the non-operational signal box on platform 2 is open for viewing and visitors are welcome to pull the levers. For many years it was situated alongside the level crossing on Station Road, as Sheringham East Box, where it controlled signals and points in that area as well as the level crossing gates. A good view can be had of the replica Eastern and Midlands Railway design water crane similar to the original that was there until the late 1960s. Watch the novel scissors mechanism in use when the engines stop here to take water.

At the Weybourne end of Holt station yard is a former Midland Railway style signal box relocated from Upper Portland Sidings near Mansfield, which has been restored to control the signals and points at southern end of the line. Beyond the signal box is another new M&GN style building, a water tower in the style of the one that was at Norwich City station.

Time to leave.
'Tickets please'.
Engine drivers.
Duckers & Divers.
No such skivers.
1 in 10 - men.
Firing, tiring.
Whose made the fire glow?
Fireman I know.
Don't smoke,
stoke.
Oily rags.
Gladrags.
Mailbags.
Then that oddity.
The Great St Trinian's Train Robbery.
Didlee-doddery, diddlee-doddery…
Stop the snobbery.
Under the bridge,
Cromer Ridge,
Kelling Heath,
beneath,
1 in 80,
matey.
Skelding Hill,
What a thrill,
Give her a fill,
Dead Man's Hill,
Weybourne Mill.
Hope, slope.
Paddington Bear.
What's his fare?
Not a care.
Lost and found.
He sleeps as sound,
As London Underground.
Didleedown, didleedown, didleedown.

She's got a ticket to ride.
Beside
Her and the porter
oughter
make for Platform 9 and three-
    quarters.
Daughters, walkers, talkers and
    deer stalkers.
Hogwart's Express?
I guess.
Dress?
Yes.

Murder on the Express.
Orient?
Not clairvoyant.
Hercule Poirot.
Yes or no?
What a sleuth.
That's the truth.
Little grey cells.
Class always tells.
Doing a ton? (Non!)
Murder mystery.
Agatha Christie!
Whodunit?
Buffet.
Fine wine.
Dine & rhyme
No plum duff.
Don't be gruff.
Huffed and puffed.
Well chuffed.
Mild and bitter?
Tommy Tripper.
Tea in the sun.
Diddledum, diddledum.
Hummm'
Sandwiches and a bun.
Not BR but freshly 'dun'…
Roaming,
In the gloaming.
Signal box.
Levers and locks.
Hitchcock's,
39 Steps
Lets.
Thrillers and killers.
Strangers on a Train. Who's to
    blame?
The Lady Vanishes.
A gover-ness.
Night Train to Munich.
Tunic.
Empress of India.
Perfidia.
Northwest Frontier.
Train to nowhere.
Ghost trainz.
Re-arranged.
Train of events.
Superin-ten-dents.
Euston…

'City of Truro' was one of ten new 4-4-0 inside cylinder locomotives ordered from the Swindon Works in 1903 and all named after towns and cities served by the Great Western Railway. In 2005 it arrived on a low-loader and was gently eased on to the tracks at Sheringham, ready to be shunted to Weybourne for final preparation and checks before going on to the Norfolk tourist track. The first train to exceed 100mph, it was soon slicing through scenic countryside at the more sedate speed of 25mph maximum but still retained all its romance and majesty.

Tootin'…rootin'…Movin'
Faster and faster.
Stationmaster.
Pullman car.
Bright star.
Ravenous?
St. Pancreas.
(Sic)
Just a trick.
…Clickety click, Clickety clop.
*Didlee-bop,did-lee-bop,didd-a-lee-*Stop!

…Mynde-the-doors!
Dogs on all fours.
All change.
Strange.
Popular resort.
Thought.
What a view.
A 'DMU'.
Freight,
wait.
Helter-skelter.
Find that Anderson shelter.
Rolling stock.
Running amok.
Don't worry,
No need to hurry.
We'll be there by 3.
In time for tea.
See the sea.
Didleedee, didleedee, didleedee.

Whistle while you work.
Never hurt.
Give a shrill.
Another fill.
Sweating, fretting,
Junction, function.
Excursion-Diversion.
Muckleburgh collection.
What a selection.
Thanks for the Tanks
Up Kelling's banks.
Sherrin'hum West.
Weybourne's best.
Bridal train.
Sweet refrain.
Loco sheds.
Weds.

Marriage in the carriage.
Closely coupled.
Untroubled.
King's Cross?
Criss-cross,
Trellis fencing.
Needs mending.
Replica?
Bet yer'.
Authenticity?
'lectricity
Spring Beck, Sherrin'hum Hall.
Why not call?
Fabled,
stabled - locos
Gabled portico's.
Kelling Woods,
Goods
Bridge Road Curve,
Swerve
Hudswell Clarke.
Sherrin'hum Park,
Up with the lark.
Humphrey Repton,
Simply perfection.
Gilding the lily.
Puffin' Billy.
Gazebo.
Off we go.
Says who?
The guard.
Working hard.
Still it's fun.
Didleedum, didleedum, didleedum.

Bridge 301.
Give it the gun.
What fun!
Heather and gorse
Golf course.
Hole in one.
Well done.
Seventh Heaven!
1 in 87.
Now that view.
Brush Type 2.
Monster from Doncaster.
Pop goes that diesel.
Favourite of the artist's easel.
What about us?

Railbus…
No fuss.
Rush. Rush.
Can't see him for dust.
Must depart.
Quad-art.
Hundred Acre Wood,
Good.
Bridge 304.
And more.
Didleedoor, didleedoor, didleedoor.

Branch no more for Blakeney, Cley
(still dry?)
and sea
or Salthouse to make a bee.
Hit that bend,
'agen'
Going around.
Slowing down.
No fault at Holt.
Titfield Thunderbolt?
Wait your time.
End of the line.
Another ice cream mum!
Didleedum, didleedum, didleedum!

From the air steam trains and the distant shores make a beautiful and timeless sight. On the landward side of the line from Sheringham to Weybourne station are woodlands forming part of the Sheringham Hall estate, which parallel the line most of the rest of the way to Weybourne station. Sheringham Hall is a Regency building, now part of the National Trust, and the garden is the work of Humphrey Repton. The grounds are open to the public all year round and in late May and early June there are magnificent displays of rhododendrons. Panoramic views of the area, including the railway, are to be seen from the gazebo in the park. A mile long footpath leads to the park from Weybourne station. Mike Page

92 Squadron heading for Holt.

The engine fireman.

No.69621 was the last of the class to be built at Stratford, being completed in March 1924. On extended loan to the railway from the East Anglian Railway Museum, its restoration was completed at Weybourne. In 2007 the N7 became one of three classic East Anglian locos (the B12, J15 being the other two) on the NNR regular service fleet. The Society's other engine, Hudswell Clarke 0-6-0T industrial tank, built in 1938 for the sugar beet factory at Wissington in the Fens, was under restoration away from the railway.

61572 steaming out of Weybourne station.

The footbridge at Weybourne was erected in 1989 following its removal from Stowmarket station due to electrification of the Norwich to London line.

Beyond bridge 303 and all the way to Weybourne station the engines have to work hard up a gradient of 1 in 80. On the seaward side a group of coastguards' cottages close to the cliff edge can be seen and then the picturesque windmill, which is now a private residence. Mike Page

J15 waiting for the signal to clear.

The standard post-1957 British Railways emblem is universally known as the 'Ferret & Dartboard'.

Opposite: The mass of pipes and controls on the footplate of No.61572.

On 9 May 1904 *City of Truro* made history by becoming the first man made creation to attain a three figure speed. Travelling between Plymouth and Paddington with driver Moses Clements at the head of the five-van 'Ocean Mails Express', it clocked 102.3mph descending Wellington Bank in Somerset but the record was kept quiet by Great Western Railway at the time, because the company feared a public backlash. The restored engine is now part of the National Railway Collection and it often tours various preservation lines including the North Norfolk Railway.

All fired up on board *92 Squadron*!

5643, a GWR 0-6-2T 5600 class locomotive normally based at the Lakeside and Haverthwaite Railway, which was borrowed by the NNR in 2007. 200 locos of this class were built and eight survive in preservation.

Passing under Bridge Road (bridge no.299) leaving Holt. On the right before the bridge, are the carriage storage sheds housing much of the railway historic rolling stock. The NNR is responsible for all the bridges on the line.

Bullied Pacific No.34081 '92 Squadron' heading for Holt thunders past Windmill Crossing, Kelling Heath, where in the past a wind-pump was used to supply water for the dwelling. The trains are limited to 25mph speed limit on the railway line.

61572 takes on water at Sheringham by bridge 305.

Beyond Kelling Heath Park Halt the line continues to climb the lengthy gradient of 1 in 80 through a deep cutting and out on to the open heathland of Kelling Heath, with heather and gorse making splashes of colour at appropriate times of the year. Occasionally, during periods of high fire risk, it may be necessary for a diesel engine to be put on the train at Weybourne for the run across the heath.

Birds eye view of Bullied Pacific No.34081 *92 Squadron* heading for Sheringham during an October morning run.

Mike Page

65462

Magnificent shadows accompany LNER N7 0-6-2T 69621 on its journey to Weybourne. To the south of Weybourne are the hills and woods of the Cromer Ridge. Mike Page

139

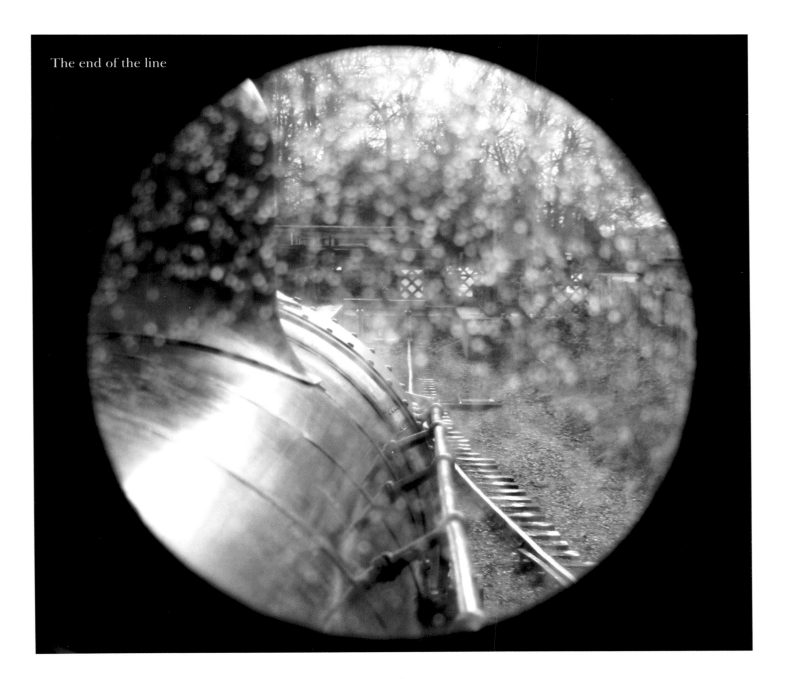

The end of the line

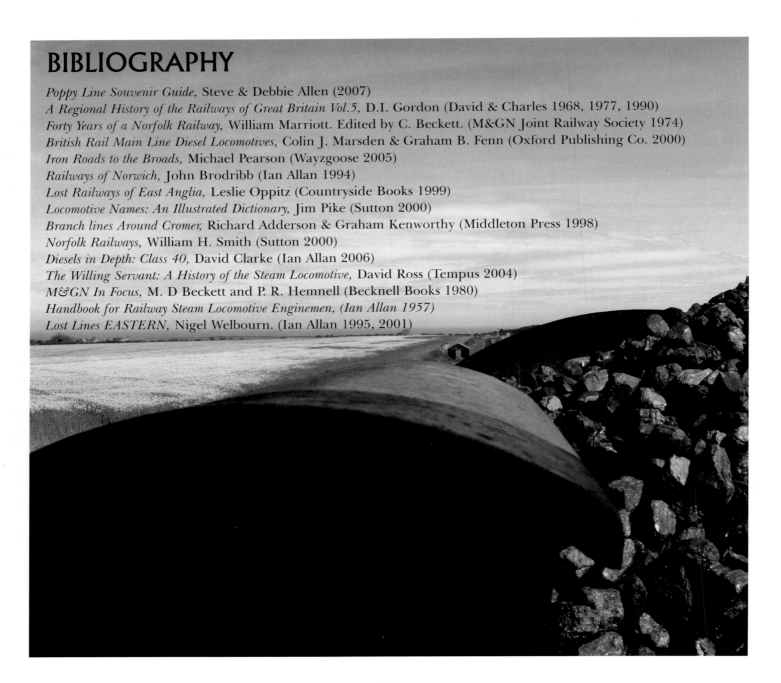

BIBLIOGRAPHY

Poppy Line Souvenir Guide, Steve & Debbie Allen (2007)

A Regional History of the Railways of Great Britain Vol.5, D.I. Gordon (David & Charles 1968, 1977, 1990)

Forty Years of a Norfolk Railway, William Marriott. Edited by C. Beckett. (M&GN Joint Railway Society 1974)

British Rail Main Line Diesel Locomotives, Colin J. Marsden & Graham B. Fenn (Oxford Publishing Co. 2000)

Iron Roads to the Broads, Michael Pearson (Wayzgoose 2005)

Railways of Norwich, John Brodribb (Ian Allan 1994)

Lost Railways of East Anglia, Leslie Oppitz (Countryside Books 1999)

Locomotive Names: An Illustrated Dictionary, Jim Pike (Sutton 2000)

Branch lines Around Cromer, Richard Adderson & Graham Kenworthy (Middleton Press 1998)

Norfolk Railways, William H. Smith (Sutton 2000)

Diesels in Depth: Class 40, David Clarke (Ian Allan 2006)

The Willing Servant: A History of the Steam Locomotive, David Ross (Tempus 2004)

M&GN In Focus, M. D Beckett and P. R. Hemnell (Becknell Books 1980)

Handbook for Railway Steam Locomotive Enginemen, (Ian Allan 1957)

Lost Lines EASTERN, Nigel Welbourn. (Ian Allan 1995, 2001)